NIGHT VISIONS

Jan L. Richardson

NIGHT VISIONS

searching the shadows of advent and christmas

—

Wanton Gospeller Press

ORLANDO, FLORIDA

Wanton Gospeller Press, Orlando, Florida
Text and illustrations © 1998 by Jan L. Richardson

Printed in China on acid-free paper

10 9 8 7 6 5 4 3 2 1

Library of Congress Cataloging-in-Publication Data for the original edition
Richardson, Jan L.
    Night visions : searching the shadows of Advent and Christmas /
Jan L. Richardson.
        p.   cm.
    ISBN 0-8298-1255-5 (alk. paper)
    1. Advent—Prayer–books and devotions—English. 2. Christmas—Prayer–books and devotions—English. 3. Epiphany—Prayer–books and devotions—English.   I. Title.
BV40.R53 1998
242'.33—dc21   97-45177
                                                                                              CIP

ISBN for this Wanton Gospeller Press edition: 978-0-9778162-3-1

wantongospeller.com   janrichardson.com

For the Tuesday Group,

whom I will always remember

gathered around the flame

CONTENTS

—

ILLUSTRATIONS

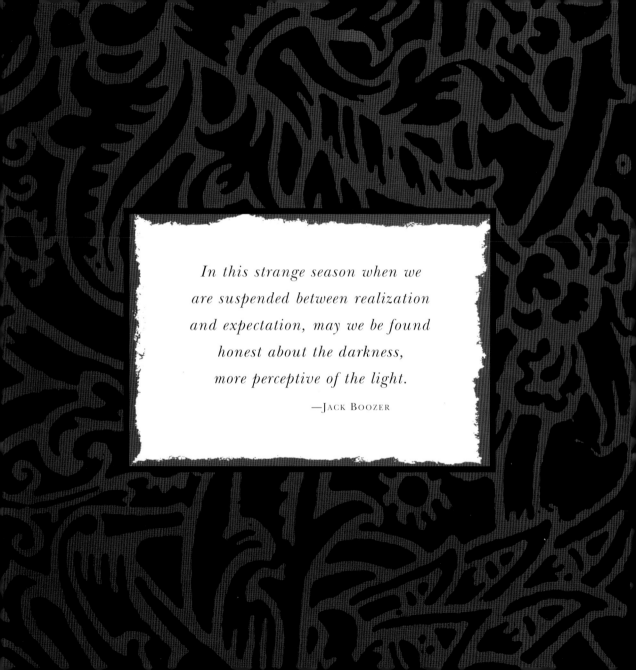

In this strange season when we
are suspended between realization
and expectation, may we be found
honest about the darkness,
more perceptive of the light.

—JACK BOOZER

ACKNOWLEDGMENTS

In creating the paper collages that appear in this book as well as writing the text, a process of piecing together took place. I believe that the way in which we create is linked to the manner in which we find patterns and make sense of the different pieces of our lives. I am grateful to many folks who have companioned me in this piecework, both in helping to fashion the book itself and in sharing the stories that gave rise to the book.

Paul Hueber, Sue Joiner, Brenda Lewis, and Judy Richardson read the manuscript and supported the writing and the writer in a variety of life-giving ways. Others who have been part of the piecework by their companionship in light and especially in shadows include Mary Ellen Barrett; Bob Bushong; Brother David Liedl, T.O.R., and the San Pedro Spiritual Development Center; Trudy Rankin; Karen Weatherford; Alice Williams; and Debby Zutter.

At United Church Press, I found gracious and gifted visionaries in Lynne Deming, Kim Sadler, Martha Clark, and Marjorie Pon.

I am grateful to J. Ruth Gendler, a true night visionary, for leading me to D. Patrick Miller's poem "Early Darkness," a portion of which appears in this book. The poem first appeared in Ruth's book *Changing Light: The Eternal Cycle of Night and Day*, a wondrous collection of myths, poems, and prayers which is now out of print. For years this book has blessed my mornings and provided benediction at night, and her work has deepened my own understanding of light and shadow.

My family has long provided safety in the shadows and fertile ground for dreams.

During my last two years as the associate pastor at St. Luke's United Methodist Church in Orlando, Florida, a group of women met in my home on a weekly basis to share and struggle through our spiritual journeys. In those nighttime conversations, they taught me a great deal about seeing in the dark. I dedicate this book to them.

horizon

The season of Advent means there is something on the horizon the likes of which we have never seen before. It is not possible to keep it from coming, because it will. That's just how Advent works. What is possible is to not see it, to miss it, to turn just as it brushes past you. And you begin to grasp what it was you missed, like Moses in the cleft of the rock, watching God's hindquarters fade in the distance.

So stay. Sit. Linger. Tarry. Ponder. Wait. Behold. Wonder.

There will be time enough for running. For rushing. For worrying. For pushing.

For now, stay. Wait.

Something is on the horizon.

INTRODUCTION

W hen I was a child, my family marked the coming of Christmas with candles. Each Sunday night of Advent we would gather by the Advent wreath in the darkened living room. I have few specific memories of what took place; I know that we read Scripture, sang a hymn, and prayed. I do remember that lighting the appropriate number of candles was a coveted responsibility shared by my sister, brother, and me. As a flame was added each week, our anticipation grew. We were drawing closer to the heart of the celebration.

In the Northern Hemisphere, Christmas falls in the dark of winter. Its roots lie in ancient festivals in which fires were kindled for light and warmth to ease the shadows and chill of the season. Growing up in the latter part of the twentieth century, with electric light so readily available, I rarely experienced utter darkness. Growing up in Florida, where Christmas is occasionally spent in air-conditioning, I had only a dim awareness of the relief that fire brings to shivering bodies. Yet in the childhood lighting of the Advent candles, something still spoke to me of mystery, of longing, of something wondrous that lay on the horizon just beyond sight. I knew that the flames heralded celebration, were portents of the festival to come.

As we lit each candle of the Advent wreath, we pieced together the story of Christmas. By the time we lit the last candle, the white center candle, on Christmas Day, we knew the end of the story. Or so we thought.

As I have grown, I have gained an appreciation for how many ways there are to tell a story. Take the story of Christmas. We can tell it as the story of an unwed mother who dared to enter into partnership with God to bring forth new life; as a political story about the birth of a revolutionary; as a tale about a love that longed so much for us that it took flesh, formed in the dark womb of a woman who shared her body and blood to bring it forth. We can tell it as a story about darkness giving birth to light, about seemingly endless waiting, and about that which lies at the end of all our waiting. Any story can be told innumerable ways, not simply according to who does the telling but to where that person is on the journey. As my life unfolds and my perspective changes, I realize that each telling of a story reveals part of the whole, but does not contain the whole story in itself. The stories I tell are continually shaped by my changing understanding of events, conversations, feelings, influences, the people around me, and of my own self. The understanding of

tell it as a story

about darkness

giving birth to

light, about

seemingly end-

less waiting, and

about that which

lies at the end of

all our waiting

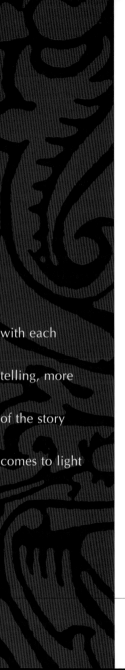

with each

telling, more

of the story

comes to light

my past continues to change according to the experiences of my present. With each telling, more of the story comes to light, even as the lighting of the Advent candles progressively leads us closer to the full blaze of Christmas.

As I have pieced together the stories and reflections contained in this book, I have come to understand them as being like candles lending light to the particular theme of each week, which was shaped by the lectionary readings for this season and by my understanding of the way this season unfolds. By itself, a daily reading would shed little light on a given theme. Taken together, the seven readings and accompanying prayers offer more illumination for the theme.

Not all the stories and reflections that I share actually occurred during the days of Advent and Christmas. They are, however, some of the stories that I carry with me in this season, that have fed my understanding of what these days mean. Darkness, desire, preparing a space, hope, birthing, welcoming, thresholds: I understand these themes not only from living through the seasons of Advent and Christmas but from living through the rest of the year as well, both in feast times and in fallow.

I carry with me the awareness that many people find that this season brings not tidings of comfort and joy but of frustration and grief. I have sought to acknowledge the shadows of this season as well as the light and to describe the ways that I find they dwell together. I believe that Christ came not to dispel the darkness but to teach us to dwell with integrity, compassion, and love in the midst of ambiguity. The one who grew in the fertile darkness of Mary's womb knew that darkness is not evil of itself. Rather, it can become the tending place in which our longings for healing, justice, and peace grow and come to birth.

Musician Suzanne Vega inspired the title of this book with her song "Night Vision" from her recording *Solitude Standing.* Sung as if to a child afraid of the dark, the song tells of the artist's longing to give the child vision to see into the night. I believe that this is the gift that God holds out to us in this season: to carry the light, yes, but also to see in the dark and to find the shape of things in the shadows, as Suzanne reminds us. With a perception that goes beyond visual sight, we are called to know and to name the gifts of the night and to share the visions that emerge from the darkness.

I write these words on the summer solstice, the longest day of the year, almost as far from Christmas as one can possibly get. Yet tomorrow the earth will begin its tilt away from the sun and the darkness will begin to wax for us in the Northern Hemisphere, drawing us closer to the mystery that lies waiting within it. In darkness and in light, God beckons us to keep vigil and to companion one another in this and every season. In giving voice to our visions, we find strength in the shadows and a presence that guides the way.

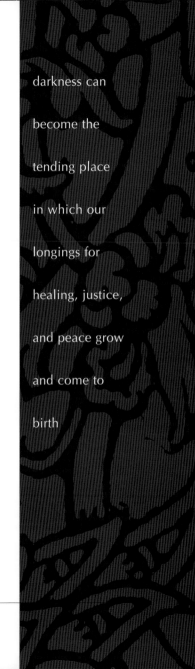

darkness can

become the

tending place

in which our

longings for

healing, justice,

and peace grow

and come to

birth

week one

DARKNESS

{ First Sunday in Advent }

You have hidden your face from us.

—Isaiah 64:7

The Advent journey begins in darkness. I am familiar with this terrain. A child of the night, a lover of stars, it is in the darkening hours that I feel most at home. Yet often we are fed the untruth that darkness is synonymous with evil and that all that is light and bright is good. At best this belief hinders us from seeing the gifts present in darkness; at worst, it encourages prejudices, however subconscious, against persons with skin darker than our own. We require darkness for birth and growth: the seed in the ground, the seed in the womb, the seed in our souls. In the dark lie possibilities for intimacy, for rest, for healing. Although we may find journeying in the dark fearsome or confusing, it teaches us to rely on senses other than sight. In the process we learn that darkness bears the capacity for good, even as evil can take place in broad daylight.

I recognize that how we feel about darkness can be a matter of privilege. To a large extent I choose what sort of darkness I live in, at least physically. I have enough money to pay my light bills, to buy candles to light every corner of my home, to keep my oil lamps full. I live in a neighborhood where I am certain that a knock on the door in the middle of the night is not a soldier come to cart me off without warning to a cell, to torture, or to death. I grew up in the country, in a home surrounded by a field where it was safe to steal outside and watch the stars until the wee hours.

2

But I know about anguish that comes as evening has fallen. I remember the phone call that came to tell of the death of a friend, and how I walked out into the night and shrieked at the shadows. I recall learning of a friend raped in the middle of the night, and how, on receiving the news, I immediately turned on my security system, lit the candles, called a friend to come spend the night with me, and lay awake long after I finally went to bed. I know the darkness of my own moods, of the shadows and sightlessness that depression brings as well as the wisdom and healing it offers when I am willing to follow its dark labyrinth.

We often find ourselves at times in the dark—good or evil or in between, of our own or another's making. Our work is to name the darkness for what it is and to find what it asks of us: whether it is darkness that asks for justice to bring the dawn of hope to a night of terror, or for a candle to give warmth to the shadows, or for companions to hold us in our uncertainty and unknowing, or for a blanket to enfold us as we wait for the darkness to teach us what we need to know.

In these Advent days of darkness and waiting, it may indeed seem that God's face is hidden from our sight. But the sacred presence is there, breathing in the shadows. This is when we learn to trust senses other than sight and to seek the face of God beneath our fingertips.

3

DARKNESS

⌐

Begin here.

Say that you have chosen it.

Say that it was your own hand that turned out the light, your own mouth that blew out the candle, your own eyes that closed themselves against the brightness.

Say it was your doing.

Say you needed the shadows, the darkness, that your eyes had begun to squint at the brightness, that the light had begun to make your head buzz. Say you needed the rest.

Say you asked for it. Longed for it.

Say you didn't.

Say it wasn't you who chose it, wasn't you who reached to turn off the light, wasn't you who snuffed out the flame, who covered your eyes.

Say the darkness stole up on you, say it overtook you, say it clamped its hand over your mouth before you could scream, its fingers across your eyes before you could take one last look at the light. Say it jimmied your door in the middle of the day, say it climbed through your window in the middle of the night and took sunrise with it.

Or say it simply called to you from where it stood in the doorway, looking longingly at you and winking its great pale eye.

Say you followed it home.

Each week's reflections begin on the Monday prior to the specified Sunday.

Move over the face of

my deep,

my darkness,

my endless restless chaos,

and create,

O God;

trouble me,

comfort me,

stir me up,

and calm me,

but do not cease

to breathe

your Spirit into

my wakening soul.

ANNUNCIATION

We sit high up on the ledge of the canyon, looking down, down, down at the patchwork of green below. Growing up in Florida, down was never very far. Here in Canada, in the far reaches of Ontario, I can't remember ever having been able to see so far down and still be touching the earth.

We sit, quiet, listening to the different ways that wind can sound when the earth encloses it nearly all the way around.

Late in the afternoon we turn back into the trees, back the way we came, and soon realize that the darkness is filtering in much more quickly than we'd planned. We had passed the threshold of evening without realizing it, so fluidly did the shadows begin to gather. We walk fast through the unfamiliar trees, and faster; I brush the back of Kary's shoulder to make certain I'm still following her. The forest noises feed our wild imaginations. Finally we burst through to the other side, sure that we have just barely managed to elude all sorts of dangers within the boundaries of the forest.

Is this what it was like, Mary, on the day of your annunciation? Listening to all the ways that wind could sound as you began to encompass it? Turning and realizing that nothing looked the same on the path you had taken? Running, running, running, reaching out your hand, praying in the darkness to brush a solid, familiar shoulder?

week one

Not to one

but to many you have called:

come

on the dancing wind

come

from the deepest forest

come

from the highest places

come

from the distant lands

come

from the edge of darkness

come

from the depth of fear

and become

the bearer of God.

CHOOSING

—

In the dream I stand at the opening. Of what, I'm not sure—a cave, perhaps, or maybe a tunnel. I tell the people with me that I don't want to go in. The space is narrow; I won't be able to breathe. This is a recurring fear, breathlessness, perhaps owing in part to the lung that collapsed repeatedly during adolescence. The collapses didn't scare me half so much as the final treatment did: tetracycline poured through a tube into my chest. They can't give you enough anesthesia to deaden the pain of acid forming scar tissue on your lung. All I remember is searing pain, the flowing acid turning into a crushing weight on my chest, leaving me barely enough breath to cry out as I mangled the hands that I gripped: the nurse's on one side, my mother's on the other.

In the dream I take a breath, pass through the opening, and am surprised to find it more spacious inside than I anticipated. I can move and breathe easily in the gaping darkness. I walk steadily through the passageway, then through another, and another. Each tunnel spills out into a clearing of light. I have to choose whether to stop in the light or to find the next dark tunnel that lies beyond.

There is never just one choice in the clearing. There are always several passageways farther along. I have to choose without seeing what's ahead. But as I take each entry step, my breath rises and falls with the realization: in the darkness, there are many ways to go.

In the daylight

we can get by on sight,

but for the nighttime

is our hearing,

There are other senses,   is our tasting,

you tell us,   is our smelling,

and when the darkness   is our questioning,

obscures our choices,   longing touching.

we must turn

to the other ways of knowing   A thousand messages waiting

you have given us.   for our sensing

                                 you have given us,

                                 O God.

SHADOW GODDESS

—

The picture I have of her is a photocopy. I can hardly tell what the original sculpture looked like, but I remember that I was less struck by the piece itself than by its title: *Shadow Goddess*. The name enchants me.

We are, most of us, taught to know a God who lives in a blaze of glory, a deity so dazzling that humans who dare to gaze upon the fiery presence rarely live to tell the tale. There is something startling about a deity who dwells also in shadow, who chooses and creates the night again and again, who hallows the waning hours. I want to know her, this presence who goes with us as day gives way to darkness.

week one

And when you have drawn

your cloak of night about you,

and when

you have rolled back

the day sky

and pinned it to the horizon,

and when

you have given yourself

to the darkness,

and when you have blurred

the familiar shapes

into uncertain shadows,

then,

thou tender of darkness

and of day,

do not forget me.

THE NIGHT I LANDED

The night I landed, I came to you, carrying fire in my hands across your new threshold. And later you held me, the flame still burning. We never turned off all the lights when we were together. There was always one lamp on, a candle burning, some brightness some-where casting shadows as we blurred the lines we had known.

It was an unspoken agreement, the lingering light. We two, who carried so much dark-ness within us in those days, didn't trust the darkness around us. And so we cast the light like some kind of anchor. I didn't know the ways the darkness would still find us, resting its fingers around my throat for months to come, casting me forth from the place I had landed.

Why did you give us

such tender skin

and ask us

to carry fire?

We are consumed

by our own smoldering,

hardly knowing

the power we carry

to scald.

Dress the wounds

we have borne

and given

from our own burning.

Make us wise

to the fire in our bones,

that it may be

for warmth and light in

all our darkness.

BLESSING FOR A LONELY NIGHT

She had me over for dinner; a lovely evening, but as I was leaving I saw sadness touch her cheek. Her sweetheart was far away. I went home and thought about missing for a while and then slipped these lines under her door the next day.

> May you befriend the darkness.
> May Sister Night be a tender and fierce companion.
> May Longing lie down with you;
> may you trace the curve of Desire's face
> and sleep in Memory's embrace.
> May the spirits attend your dreaming
> till absence gives way to flesh
> and the shadows return your touch.

When you have thrown

the cloak of evening

across me,

and when you have drawn

your midnight hand

across my face;

when you have made my soul

as dark as the nighttime sky,

and when the shadows

are my only companions;

then, O God,

turn my face upward,

that I may know

the grace of stars

and give myself to rest.

week one

THE NEW BOWL

I hold the bowl, the new bowl I bought today. Midnight blue on the outside, white on the inside, it fits into the palms of my two hands. A good weight. Its size will accommodate food enough to sustain me through the evening, through sleep, through dreams.

Washing it by hand late that night, I remember a shred from a D. Patrick Miller poem.

There is no dying of the light—
just the washing of a bowl,
and overturning it for night.

I rinse the new bowl, turn it over in the drainer, and sink into the night.

In the turning of the bowl

is the turning of the world,

and in every moment

somewhere

the day is turning to darkness.

week one

Bless those who welcome it,

who long for it;

bless those who fear it

and bid it quickly pass.

And those who touch

with delight in the night,

bless;

and those who cry out

as the shadows give way

to terror,

bless too.

Make us bold

in the darkness

to protect each other's slumber,

and make us courageous

in the night

to guard each other's dreams.

week two

DESIRE

{ Second Sunday in Advent }

How I long for all of you.

—Philippians 1:8

Each year, early in the fall, the voices begin clamoring to tell us what we want. We cannot go shopping, read the newspaper, listen to the radio, or watch television without being told what will make our holidays complete. Toys for our children (if we have them), jewels for our partners (if we have them), presents for our coworkers (if we have a job), lavish food for the family holiday meal (if we have family, if they live close enough, if we even want to be with them). We rail at the commercialism of Christmas even as we sometimes get caught up in it.

But the voices will never tell us what we really want, what we really long for, what we desire with heart and soul. Those who have sat in the darkness know how the shadows give way to desire. Without sight, without our heads swimming with the images of what others tell us we want, we can turn our gaze inward and search our souls. What speaks to us? What calls to us? What dreams have we buried? What wounds cry out for healing? What longs to be born in us in this season? What is the yearning which we have not dared to name? Our desires reveal to us what we think about God, about ourselves, and about the world.

In her remarkable book of prayers entitled *All Desires Known,* Janet Morley writes, "I understand the Christian life to be about the integration of desire: our personal desires, our political vision, and our longing for God. So far from being separate or in competition with one another, I believe that our deepest desires ultimately spring from the same source." Advent offers the opportunity to explore that source, to discern our desires and to find their common ground.

In this season, I journey with questions: What and whom do I desire? Do my desires spring from a longing for wholeness or from a sense of inadequacy? Do they come from within me or from what others say I should want? Will the things I long for bring healing to others as well as to myself? Will my desires draw me closer to God? Do I really believe the Holy One desires me, loves me unconditionally, longs for me?

The one who invited Mary into partnership assures us that we, too, are desired and desirable. So desired, we are invited to claim our own desires and to name the longings that we carry in this season.

HOW THE WEATHER WAS

All good books are alike in that . . . after you are finished reading one you will feel that all that happened to you and afterwards it all belongs to you: the good and the bad, the ecstasy, the remorse and sorrow, the people and the places and how the weather was.

—ERNEST HEMINGWAY

Your words arrive as I am in the midst of painting my bedroom. They tell me your version of what I have known in my gut for some time. The slow erosion becomes landslide, your words turning to rain that hollows out my terrain.

I had moved into my studio when I began to paint my bedroom, and now I take to that space in earnest. Always my favorite room, it becomes an ark in this torrential weather. I go to bed early and read for hours, curled up on the futon. The books pile up, encircling me, enfolding me, giving me words I cannot yet find on my own. I am drawn to stories of women in the wilderness, women on the prairie, women of the land who staked their claims and widened their boundaries, women who survived. I find myself fascinated by the stories of women who live in the arid West. I long for their weather, for the dryness that enfolds them, for relief from this torrent that drenches my bones.

I will never return

to my original landscape,

I know;

the currents forever change

the lay of my land,

and the tides ever shift

my bones.

But for a moment, God,

gather up

the water-soaked skirts

you drag across my terrain,

and let me see

the curves of my soul

undisturbed by the torrents

that wash through my days.

week two

PATTERNS

—

Kary sends me bits and pieces of patterns from halfway around the world. Postcards and envelopes postmarked New Zealand bear to me photos of fabrics she has collected, vivid papers, scraps of textures, colors, lines. I lay them out on my table, arrange and rearrange them, turn them in my hands. I pray the patterns will pierce my eye, settle in my brain, rework the lines that tunnel my field of vision.

Long ago she told me she takes a dim view of always making patterns match. Delight comes in the unlikeliest pairings, she said. Comfort arrives in changing the rules.

Forgive us, God,

when we live our lives

within the lines,

when we say

this is the shape of our

work

this is the boundary of our   Draw us beyond our patterns

habitation   into yours:

these are the limits to our   shifting, moving,

love   curving, spiraling,

these are the lines of our   many-colored, ever-changing,

vision   stretching, pushing,

these, and none other.   challenging, renaming,

                                      unsettling, disturbing,

                                      casting forth,

                                      and welcoming home.

week two

25

FROM PASSION TO PASSION

—

As she tells me goodnight, she says the birds might wake me in the morning. I tell her this is no problem; it's been ages since I've been awakened by birds. It's not that we don't have them in the suburbs of Orlando. It's just that I wouldn't leave my windows open through the night the way that I do here in this house on the side of a mountain in North Carolina.

I fall asleep thinking about birds and how, as a young child, I wanted to become an ornithologist when I grew up. "Oh, you want to study fish!" one of my elementary school teachers said when I told the class. "No," I said patiently. "Birds."

When I was seven I wrote to the Jacksonville Zoo and asked if they would send me some bird feathers. Soon after that, a large manila envelope arrived for me in the mail. It was filled with beautiful feathers of all sizes and colors. It had been sent by a man who said he was the bird curator, and I still imagine him walking around the cages at the zoo, looking for feathers to send to a seven-year-old girl who loved birds. His name was John True. I still remember that and wonder what became of him.

I cannot remember what gave rise so long ago to that seven-year-old girl's consuming fascination with birds, or exactly when it was that her drawings of birds that she hung on the walls gave way to pictures of Shaun Cassidy. I have wanted to be many things since dreaming of becoming an ornithologist, but the intense focus with which I pursued that interest shaped every intention that would follow.

The next morning, there in North Carolina, I wake early to the sound of birds through the open window. I lie for a long time in the bed and think about how in my life I have moved from passion to passion, but at least two abide: my longing for nesting, my yearning for flight.

God of the open window,

the star-drenched sky,

the gathering dawn;

God of every creature

that takes flesh

and form

from your own desire;

when night is at its deepest,

may I know

the comfort of home

beneath

your welcoming wing,

that when day

comes to the window,

I may gather up my dreams

and fly.

SOFT SHEETS

I bought the sheets during a lonely spell. They looked like the colors of my soul, warm and deep and welcoming. But after I washed them and spread them on my bed and lay down on them that night, they began to mock me. I called Kary, weeping. "I'm so lonely and these sheets are so scratchy and it takes so long for one person to make sheets soft!" I wailed. It was like a Zen koan: What is the sound of one hand clapping? How does one person make sheets soft?

Her voice was soothing, and I slept. Night turned into day turned into another night, and after a long while of this I called her back. "I woke up this morning and realized my sheets were soft," I said.

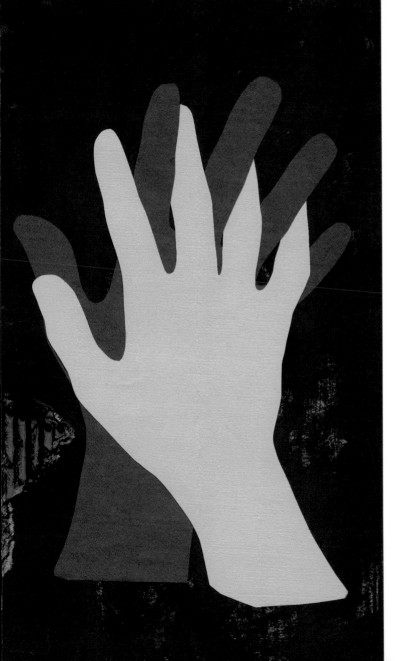

Beloved companion,

you are my delight,

but sometimes I need you

to take flesh

and form,

to feel the breath of you

on my neck,

the hem of your garment

thrown across me

when the night

is at its darkest

and the land

has turned to sleep.

THE MOON IS ALWAYS WHOLE

I walk with Kary under a full moon on the grounds of the only castle in New Zealand. Under its light I tell her about a Barbara Kingsolver poem I have recently come across: "Remember the Moon Survives." It does, Kingsolver writes. Around the encroaching darkness the moon bends herself, curls herself and waits. Against the waxing and waning shadow, she writes, the moon is always whole.

Kary asks me if I believe this, believe in the constant wholeness of the moon. I think about the year past, about the rising and falling tide of sorrow that has played on my shores. I think of how I embraced the opportunity for this trip to another land and the possibility for respite it would provide. But the tides run in this Southern Hemisphere as well, and I am dismayed by the flow of memory that pulls me even here. I had thought to leave your shadow across the ocean.

But here, beneath the full moon, I tell Kary yes. Yes, the moon survives. Beneath the ebb and flow of darkness it is waiting. I have seen it whole.

week two

God of the two lights,

I love the sun,

its revealing brilliance,

its lingering warmth;

but in the dark of night,

let me learn

the wisdom of the moon,

how it waxes and wanes

but does not die,

how it gives itself

to shadow,

knowing it will emerge whole

once more.

ALL THE WAYS I AM WORDS

—

Almighty God, unto whom all hearts be open, all desires known, and from whom no secrets are hid . . .
    —THE BOOK OF COMMON PRAYER

Prayer book
I am
longing
for hands
tracing my spine
knowing desire
unloosing the binding
as my pages fall open.

Holy writ
I am
sacred text waiting
for you to linger over me
your fingers smoothing
the lines.

Brittle bitter ancient scroll
I am
sweet to your mouth
like Ezekiel's
and equally hard
to digest.

Story by the fire
I am
uttered again and again
changing with each telling
in the dancing flames.

On the tip of your tongue
I am
dwelling
laughing
the unsettled word
in the curves of your
        mouth.

There are stories

embedded in our skin

and words enfleshed in us,

and so may you bless us

with those who by tender touch

release the tales,

trace the lines,

free the words

one by one.

Give to us those

who will listen us

into our own language

till we are hoarse with the telling

and with the laughter

at being released

from the silences we had kept

so long.

FOR DAVID, WHO KNOWS THE VALUE OF BREAD

Just this
(for now):
that the loaves
kneaded
in your contemplative
creating,
offered as gift
in my
needed
waiting,
tasted
oh my
of grace rising,
manna delighting.

week two

You meet us in our hungering

with manna not of our making,

and in our thirsting

you surprise us

with unexpected wine.

You are the source

of our desiring

and the end

of all our longing.

O giver of the feast

and ever-present guest,

blessed be.

week three

PREPARING A SPACE

{ Third Sunday in Advent }

See, I am sending my messenger ahead of you,
who will prepare your way before you.

—MATTHEW 11:10

friend called from south Florida during Advent one year. "Go get a tree!" she said. "We're coming up to help you decorate!" Undecided up to that point as to how much energy I would put into preparing my home for the holidays that year, her call prompted me to action. I phoned Brenda and enlisted her aid in finding a tree. My staff Christmas party fell on the only night that my south Florida friends could come up, and during my absence they and Brenda borrowed a saw from one of my neighbors whom I didn't even know, hacked away at the stump of the tree till it fit the stand, wrestled it inside the house, and strung the lights. By the time I arrived home, all that remained was the pleasure of decorating and the stories of all they had had to do to prepare the tree without me.

The season of Advent is a season of preparation, a time of getting ready for what lies ahead. In Matthew's Gospel, Jesus says of John the Baptist, "This is the one about whom it is written, 'See, I am sending my messenger ahead of you, who will prepare your way before you.'" And in another Advent reading, Isaiah proclaims to us, "In the wilderness prepare the way of the Lord, make straight in the desert a highway for our God" (Isaiah 40:3). While both Matthew and Isaiah draw our attention to the horizon from which the Holy One will appear, they also draw our gaze to the path itself.

{week three: preparing a space}

This season beckons me to ask, what am I preparing for? What is the way that is being prepared within the wilderness of my life? What does it mean for my own life to become a path, a way of welcome for the Holy One? How do I give myself time to notice the ways that the path unfolds before me and within me? What are the acts of preparation that bring delight to my daily life? Whom do I ask or allow to help me prepare?

Chances are, if we don't enjoy the process of getting ready, we won't enjoy the event we are getting ready for. If we become so consumed by getting Christmas right—the right present, the right cards mailed to the right people at the right time, the right dishes for Christmas dinner—we risk missing the surprising ways that God prepares *us* in this season. As we open to God's guiding in these Advent days, we may discover that the space being prepared for the coming birth lies within our own selves.

{week three: preparing a space}

STRIPPING

I am standing in the foyer of my home. It is my threshold, my entryway, the welcoming place to all that lies within. For nearly three years I have lived in this house, this four-bedroom parsonage-for-one. So much bigger than I need. My possessions slowly began to fill this space; my soul has taken longer to stretch out here. Too many nights of rattling around in the emptiness. I remember early on, shortly after moving here, receiving an invitation from friends to come to their home blessing. I was troubled that I couldn't go, too far away; I was more troubled by how it touched all the raw places in me. I had a house; what I wanted was a home that I, too, could bless. That night I walked around my house, weeping and screaming, "I want

to go home!" But I didn't know where home was. I had left it to come here.

I am standing in the foyer, on the threshold, remembering how at home I once felt with you—how welcomed, how blessed. How the space between us helped me endure creating a space here.

I am standing in the foyer, on the threshold, at the beginning of my third Advent here. Friends are coming for New Year's, and I want to strip the faded wallpaper and paint the walls before they arrive. Removing the wallpaper is taking forever because the walls weren't properly prepared. I am reduced to soaking it and removing it shred by tiny shred. I hate the obvious connections. Each shred beneath what's left of

my fingernails reminds me how I wasn't
ready, how futile it was to try to find a
home in someone else without first finding
it inside myself. Each soggy piece whis-
pers, *Told you, told you, told you.* I strip the
walls until they are completely bare, run
my hands over the unavoidable scars left
behind. The worst of the work is done.

God of making

and unmaking,

of tearing down

and re-creating,

you are my home

and habitation,

my refuge

and place of dwelling.

In your hollows

I am re-formed,

given welcome

and benediction,

beckoned to rest

and rise again,

made ready

and sent forth.

{ day two }

IN THE MARY, MOTHER OF GOD CHAPEL

—

From the moment I stepped into this
chapel, it felt like home. Wood, stone,
glass, and flame together breathed a silent
welcome. I come here for its quiet, for its
enveloping of my soul, for the way it has
settled here amidst the green. I walk in and
know I join the unbroken worship of those
who have passed through here: the
Franciscan friars who hallow this space
with their prayers morning and evening, as
well as the persons, like me, who come
with often unnameable longings. I have
been grateful for the unseen hands that
tend this space, that change the wall hanging with each season, that place the icon in
the corner, that care for the perpetual
flame.

On this day, after the quiet, I
encounter Brother David as I leave the
chapel. I have caught him pulling the trap-
pings of Advent from the storage closet. He
is looking slightly frazzled and uses phrases
like "If Advent happens . . ." as we talk. I
know what he means. We both know
Advent will happen, with or without us.
But as people who work for religious insti-
tutions, our sacred seasons are usually the
most frenzied. For us the trick, the chal-
lenge, lies in finding ways to savor the season in the midst of the rush instead of
winding up exhausted, having missed it as
we sought to make it meaningful for others.

On this day, heading into the season, I
am grateful for the grace of our encounter.

After this ragged year gone, I gladly take
our visit as an omen, a talisman to carry
through the holy days ahead. Now I know
who prepares this space, in season and out.
The unseen hands have taken flesh, inti-
mating incarnation, pointing the way to the
coming Christ.

week three

For all the generations

that have prepared the way;

for all the unseen hands

that have made ready

every space;

for those who light

the fires of welcome

and who tend

to every resting place,

O God of every pilgrim,

we bless you with our thanks.

{ week three: preparing a space }

VESSELS

I measure my life in vessels. They trace the contours of my days. Teacup, bowl, oil lamp, pitcher, baptismal font, Communion chalice, basin, bathtub. I sleep in the belly of night and wake under a downturned bowl of blue.

I ponder their shapes as I begin to understand my own longing: wanting to be held, fighting against being contained.

Teach me, I say. Tea, food, oil, water, wine, stars, sky. Teach me how to gracefully, powerfully fill my space.

You hollow us out, God,

so that we may carry you,

and you endlessly fill us

only to be emptied again.

Make smooth our inward spaces

and sturdy,

that we may hold you

with less resistance

and bear you

with deeper grace.

M A P S

I love maps. I don't always read them incredibly well, mind you. Just last night I spent a great deal of time traveling the unfamiliar streets of Nashville because I was feeling more game for adventure than for dealing with the map. But I like to look at maps, especially the really old ones. The ones made by people who understood map-making as an art. The ones made before all the corners of the earth had been charted, and adventurous souls approaching the boundaries of the known world were warned by the cartographer's hand, "Beyond here be dragons."

I like maps for their notion of order, for their presupposition that the lines, direc-tions, and paths they offer will show us the

way if properly read. It is a heartening thought that if we study a piece of paper long enough, it will show us the way to our destination. Most of us these days live, I think, with a sense that we've wandered beyond the known world, that we're making the path as we go, with the breath of drag-ons hot on our necks.

I also think, though, that we come into the world with a scrap, a shred of some cosmic map in our grasp. It's lined onto the palms of our hands that emerged with us, fisted, from our mother's ocean. There are days when I believe that if we touch enough hands, place them side by side, we'll finally see the map. Across the land-scape of our palms, across the terrain of

our hands that come in different sizes and
colors and have wrinkles or scars and are
smooth or leathery with work and are missing fingers or are twisted with illness,
across their flesh lie the lines that if we
look closely enough are connected and will
tell us which way to go.

week three

At the edges of our borders

you wait,

and at our territorial lines

you linger,

because the place where

we touch

beyond our boundaries

is where you take

your delight.

And when we learn to read

the landscape of our fears,

and when we come to know

the terrain of every sorrow,

then will we turn

our fences into bridges

and our borders

into paths of peace.

WORKING ON IT

—

This is the waiting season. But I don't want to talk about waiting. I am sick of it.

I am riding with Lesley to the airport to fly back home. She knows how tired I am. She tells me that her therapist says that being sick and tired means you're working on it.

I don't want to work on it anymore. I am sick of working on it and not feeling better, only feeling more adept at knowing where I am torn.

I feel like I've been flayed this week, all the wounds ripped open in my return to this familiar but unsettling place. Getting out of Lesley's car, I am raw. Walking through the airport, I am smooth white bones. Taking off, I am hollowness ascending, emptiness in flight.

OFFERINGS

The television commercials, the newspaper and magazine advertisements, the Christmas displays that go up in stores long before Halloween have much invested in Christmas as a joyous season. A profitable one at least, my cynicism tells me. I could go on about how they twist the truth, throw off our timing, contribute to our frenzy in the season instead of our wonder. I could also acknowledge that marketing never exists in a vacuum, that some of us who complain about the commercialism of Christmas have occasionally contributed to the care and feeding of the Christmas beast rather than the taming of it.

But I only want, here, to ask this question: Why is there so much Lent in Advent? In this season of joy, why do I bump up against my wounds? The wise ones who journey with me remind me that there are cycles of shedding before there is conception, that birthing is painful and messy and loud, and that we find it so hard to let go, to open so that new life can emerge.

When I encounter the Lenten days of Advent, the days that beckon me to let go, I struggle to remember that I have done this before. Something within me knows about release. My body does it constantly and is renewed, letting go of flecks of skin, strands of hair, sweat, tears, blood, breath. These, too, are offerings: giving up, letting go, shedding what is not needful for the birth, making way for that which waits to be born.

These days bathe us in images

of abundance and happiness,

but we pray for those

who do not find in this time

a season of goodness

and light.

Give us eyes to see

into the shadows

cast by the millions of

blinking lights;

ears to listen

beyond the carols

to hear

the anguished weeping;

and hearts that long

for the liberation

your advent truly brings.

ORDINARY TIME

I don't care what the church calendar says, there is ordinary time in this season too. There is waking, working, talking, eating. There is sweeping, shopping, washing dishes, laundry. There is checking all the doors and windows before bed. There is turning down the covers. There is sleeping. There is rest.

week three

Still me

until I hear your heartbeat

quiet me

until I feel your breathing

make me

one with your rhythms

move me

to the cadence of your love.

week four

HOPE

{ Fourth Sunday in Advent }

Blessed is she who believed that there would be a fulfillment of what was spoken to her.

—LUKE 1:45

A seed in the ground. A flame in the darkness. A hand outstretched. A child in the womb. Hope starts small and overtakes us, stretching the borders of what we have known.

One "yes" to an angel, and Mary becomes a revolutionary. The child is hardly noticeable in her womb when she arrives at the home of her kinswoman Elizabeth, but the transformation is written all over her face, and Elizabeth instantly intuits what has happened. She blesses Mary for her hope, for her radical belief that God will fulfill the promise made by Gabriel. Elizabeth, pregnant in her advanced years, knows the power of hope. She, too, carries it in her womb.

Her ears ringing with Elizabeth's blessing, Mary pours out a song, a cry of hope that echoes the one raised by her foremother Hannah after giving birth to Samuel. The powerful brought down from their thrones! The lowly raised up! The hungry filled with good things! The rich sent away empty! But Mary sings about these things as though they have already happened! A tiny child in her womb, and God has transformed the world? What sort of outrageous hope is this?

Mary knows in her soul, in her womb, that radical hope is found at the boundary where the outrageous gives way to the possible. A child given to her aged kinswoman? The courage to say yes to Gabriel's invitation to her, an unwed woman? Well, then God might as well have turned the world into one where all things are possible! Even justice. Even freedom.

Mary knows that some things are so outrageous that sometimes we have to talk about them as if they have already happened in order to believe they could ever come about. And so if we believe that God has brought justice to the world, we live that justice, and we share in making the world more just. If we believe that God has brought healing to the world, we live that healing, and we share in making the world more whole.

Hope starts small, even as a seed in the womb, but it feeds on outrageous possibilities. It beckons us to step out with the belief that the action we take will not only bear fruit but that in taking it, we have already made a difference in the world. God invites us, like Mary, to open to God's radical leading, to step out with sometimes inexplicable faith, trusting that we will find sustenance. "Hope," writes W. Paul Jones in *Trumpet at Full Moon,* "is the simple trust that God has not forgotten the recipe for manna." The hope of God contains the promise that we will be fed, even if we never see the fruit of our hope-filled actions.

FESTIVAL OF LIGHTS

——

We are dancing in the streets of the city of my college years. The downtown is lit up for the holidays, and the music blares as our feet repeatedly hit the hard surface of the street. Tomorrow we will long for hot baths to soak the soreness from our legs, but tonight we are dancing at the Festival of Lights.

In the years to come I will learn how necessary it is to keep dancing, how celebration is not a luxury but a staple of life, how in the grimmest moments I will need to take myself down to the closest festival at hand. I will go not to drown my sorrow or to mask my despair or to ignore the real suffering of the world or of my own self. I will go to beat out the message with my feet that in the darkness we are dancing, and while we are weeping we are dancing, and our legs are aching but we are dancing. And under the night sky we are dancing; lighting a match to the shadows, we are dancing; starting to sing when they have stopped the music, we are dancing; sending shock waves with our feet to the other side of the world, we are dancing still.

Bless the feet that dance

    in Guatemala

    in El Salvador

in the midst of the night

    in Nicaragua

    in Argentina

stamping out the message

    in South Africa

    in Liberia

we will be free.

Bless the hands that clap

    in Haiti

    in Rwanda

the rhythm of liberation

    in Palestine

    in Bosnia

that light a match in the dark

    in you

    in me

and carry the coming dawn.

week four

KNEADING HOPE

I lie down with a sigh of relief. I am back in Atlanta, and it has proved to be a difficult week. Places, people, events light torches to memories left there. Betsey comes to give me a massage. Her familiar hands are a trusted blessing.

She asks what she can be pondering during our time together. I take a deep breath and think. "That my body is a good thing," I tell her. "That I can be whole."

I have been dismayed by the ache my body has carried, by the anger that flashes without warning at your remembered touches. Sleep, always an easy friend, comes with difficulty. My silences emerge as tightness gripping my throat and chest.

Beneath her touch, I rest. When I get up from the table, there will be more to face, but here, for the first time, in this pained place, I feel a tangible hope kneaded back into my body. Mistrustful skin, tender muscles, weary bones open at last in prayer, in blessing, in benediction.

I rise and go my way.

Our bodies carry scars

not visible to the naked eye,

but they are there,

telling the stories

our lips hesitate to utter

of how we settled for less

than you longed for us

to know.

We hunger for the touch

that reminds us

we are in your image,

and we ache

for the tender knowing

that hallows flesh

and soul,

that honors the sacredness

of skin

and reminds us

we are whole.

week four

THE STORY BLANKET

—◆—

When you moved into your new place, I wanted to make something welcoming for your walls. So I wove you a story, laid it out on a blanket of paper, stitched in between the lines, decorated it with layers and strands of blue, of green, of gold. This was how it went:

Once upon a nighttime, on visits back to the home where I grew up, I used to steal outside with a blanket, spread it out, and watch the stars as they passed through the gates of night. An oak tree kept me company, barren save for the moon it sometimes held in its branches. Together we bore quiet witness to the stars' journeys. The tree is gone now, but a blanket will do when one is longing for home. Spread it out and turn your gaze toward the sky. And if you haven't enough dark to see the stars, wrap the blanket about you, close your eyes, and dream yourself home.

I didn't know till much later how much I would need the story for myself. But finally I learned that I had all the time in the world, and so I wrapped the blanket around my own shoulders and closed my eyes until I could see all the stars in my own sky.

When I scan other skies

for signs of hope,

and when I walk other paths

with a longing for home,

God of the exile,

lead me back

through my own door.

Tell me

my forgotten stories,

feed me

the words I have given away,

and draw my gaze

from the far horizon

that I may see the lights

in my own sky.

HOPE'S DISGUISES

So many things disguise themselves as hope. So much crosses our threshold, promising change or relief from present circumstances, that sometimes it becomes difficult to tell the difference between a reasonable hope and a misguided delusion. My mailbox, television, and radio offer an endless stream of the latter. Thin thighs in thirty days! Fabulous wealth with no effort! A whole new image in a can of soda! The more damaging delusions are also more insidious, though they may be cloaked in good intentions. Like the night he said *I miss you* and took my hand. How could I have known at the time that that sentence had about as much promise as *You may have already won a million dollars?*

I must admit, I have sometimes lived for months on a good delusion. It will never do for staple food, but sometimes it gets me by. At least until I get to the point where I can handle the truth, as simple or as complex as it may be: My thighs are just fine. Wealth generally takes more hard work than luck. Any given soda will improve my image only to those who find themselves attracted to the belching it causes. And he may miss me, but this time I won't get drawn in.

Hope becomes easier to recognize when we learn that it rarely comes from outside us. More often it comes from within, emerging from the place where our deepest longings meet our willingness to make them real. In that place hope sheds its disguises, moving with grace and freedom to point us beyond our delusions toward the landscape of possibility.

week four

We see the signs

but cannot always

divine their meanings.

You call us to move forward

not always knowing

whether what we grasp

in our hands

will prove to be

a seed of hope

or a thorn in our flesh.

Train our fingers,

that what brings life

we may with persistence hold,

and that which wastes

our souls

we may with grace release.

QUICKENING

Is this what it feels like? Sudden fires being lit inside me. Movement I have never known. Something stealing into my awareness, being knit together in the endless darkness. An unseen but tangible wholeness.

Connie finds me at church, tells me she is pregnant, tells me she has just begun the second trimester. When she hugs me, I can feel her growing belly against mine. *A whole new world,* I think, and do not know if I mean for her or for me.

This restless hope

is what drives me

beyond the weariness

beyond the discomfort

beyond every thought

that what I carry within me

will never come to birth.

This restless hope

beyond all reason

flutters beneath my heart

and grows within my soul.

It is beyond me,

and it is of me,

and it is delivering me

home.

THE VIRGIN

(to mary)

She told me that *virgin* really means *a woman unto herself, a whole woman, a soul mother.* What a shift from thinking that a virgin is what you are until you are made complete by a man.

They still argue, Mary, about whether you were a virgin. Maybe it's never bothered me because something deep inside me knew the truth: that you were whole, that you were a woman unto yourself, that you chose freely, that you were a soul mother, a spirit catcher, a God bearer even before you consented to open your womb.

And so they can dicker over the question until the second coming, but what I really want to know is, do we want to be whole? Do we want to be healed? Because that's what Advent is asking us: Are we ready to be born?

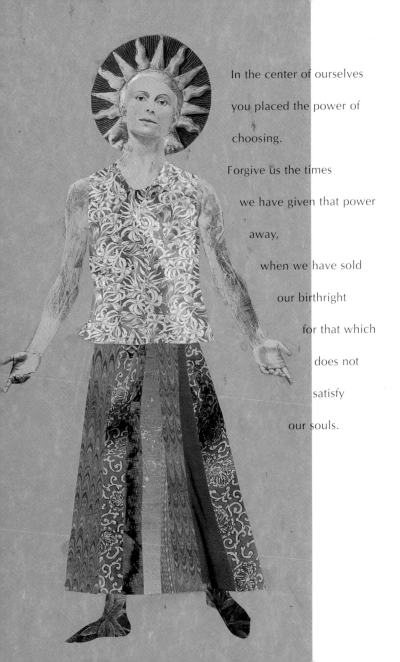

In the center of ourselves

you placed the power of

choosing.

Forgive us the times

we have given that power

away,

when we have sold

our birthright

for that which

does not

satisfy

our souls.

And so

in your wisdom

may our yes

be truly yes

and our no

be truly no,

that we may

touch with dignity

and love with integrity

and know the freedom

of our own choosing

all our days.

WOMAN, WAITING

Except that it is not visible
to the naked eye
all the ways she has ceased to wait.
They cannot see in her
that her waiting carries no idleness,
no passiveness.
She is not resigned,
awaiting the delivery of her sealed fate.
It has little to do with patience.

Her waiting has not been
a biding of time
but an abiding in time,
dwelling,
making herself at home.

She has taken every last frayed end,
knotted it;
every loose thread,
woven it;
every jagged edge,
worn it smooth;
every ragged scrap,
stitched it up.

This woman, waiting,
is the wise maiden with oil in plenty,
the grown woman who knows
the time of birthing,
the aged crone who feels in her flesh
the measure of her days.

It cannot be seen in her
all the ways she is ready.
But soon,
in the fullness of time,
she will cry out
and be delivered.

week four

Guardian of the seasons,

keeper of every time,

tune us so to your rhythms

that we may know

the occasion for stillness

and the moment for action.

May we be so prepared

so aware

so awakened

in our waiting

that when you prompt us

into motion,

our hands may be your hands

and our purposes

your own.

week five

BIRTHING

{ Christmas Day or

First Sunday after Christmas }

The time came for her to deliver her child.

—LUKE 2:6

I write this as I sit on my patio in Florida on a gorgeous spring day. We just celebrated Easter two days ago, and I find evidence of resurrection and new life all around. From here I can see that the sweet gum tree in my backyard has just started to sprout new green leaves. The crepe myrtle, cut back several months ago, has begun to show buds.

In the Northern Hemisphere, we celebrate Advent and Christmas in the midst of winter, when spring has long gone underground and new life remains stubbornly dormant. In the thick of winter, it becomes more difficult to discern what is waiting to come to life, what is longing to be born.

The festival of Christmas offers a winter thaw, an opportunity to ponder new birth when the landscape around us, and perhaps within us, seems lifeless. The celebration of Christ's birth beckons us to consider what has lain dormant in our own lives, and what new life lies waiting beneath the surface. As women and as men, during this season we share with Mary and Joseph in giving birth to the holy. Bringing forth the sacred depends not solely on the physical ability to give birth. Although that is one way to share in creating with God, we give birth, too, when we create with our hands, offer hospitality, work for justice, or teach a child. We share in giving birth whenever we freely offer ourselves for healing, for delight, for transformation, for peace. And we become, as German mystic

Meister Eckhart wrote in the Middle Ages, "mothers of God, for God is always needing to be born."

Even as we share in the joy of giving birth, we remember that birthing is a difficult and often dangerous undertaking. The child, or the hope, or the dream that we carry may not come to term. It may die. It may not look or act as we had hoped. It may require more labor in the birthing or more care in the living than ever we imagined, leaving us exhausted and drained. This is why it is so important to have midwives in the process, to have people who will attend us in our labor and beyond. To survive the labor, we need companions who will breathe with us, groan with us, hold us in the struggle, and celebrate with us even when the birthing does not go as planned. We need sisters and brothers who will encourage us to rest when we are tired, eat when we are hungry, and weep when we are grieving, that we may be strengthened to encourage and labor with others when the occasion arises. In so doing, we not only give birth but are ourselves born anew.

HER GLORIOUS ROBE

—

I am thinking of the woman clothed with the sun, the moon beneath her feet. She is pregnant and "crying out in birth pangs," Revelation 12 tells me, "in the agony of giving birth." The King James Version offers language even more ominous. "Travailing in birth," it says of the woman described in John's vision, "and pained to be delivered." The dragon lies waiting to devour her child.

For most of my life, I did not know this woman. I never learned about her in Sunday school, never heard her mentioned from the pulpit. Although the Roman Catholic tradition lifts up her story on the Feast of the Assumption of Mary, she does not appear among the scripture readings appointed in the Protestant lectionary, not even in this season fraught with images of pregnancy, hope, longing, labor, birthing. As much as anybody, I inherited the Protestant squeamishness over the Book of Revelation. I bought into my tradition's frequent willingness to leave the book to those who pick through it for signs of the end times or for fodder for the hellfire and damnation they use to scare people into their version of the realm of God. It is confusing, yes, so cloaked in language and symbols better understood by the writer's contemporaries than by us. But it is hopeful, too, literally pregnant with images of transformation and deliverance for those who live in pain and travail, with the dragon lurking at the door.

The woman clothed with the sun haunts me, journeys with me in this season. She whom God delivered, she who had a place prepared for her in the wilderness, she whom the earth came to aid, she holds out her garment to us. To those who cry out in agony, to those in travail and pained to be delivered, to those struggling toward freedom with the dragon's breath hot on their necks, she holds forth her fiery raiment, her dazzling cloak, her glorious robe.

In your mercy

clothe me

in your protection

cloak me

in your care

enfold me

in your grace

array me.

With your justice

dress me

for your labor

garb me

by your love

envelop me

and fit me

for your work.

{ day two }

HOW HE COMES

For months I had gone without Communion. Working for week after week with abused women, I had suddenly realized that I couldn't celebrate the broken body, the shed blood. So for months I fasted from Communion, and pondered, and prayed, trying to figure out in a new way what it meant.

Sitting with a group of friends coming to the end of a shared journey, I listen as they tell their stories of the years spent together. The struggles, the celebrations, the questions, the hopes. I listen as Helen, taking bread and wine, begins to weave together the stories. I listen as she transforms the strands into a blessing for the feast. I listen until I will no longer remember what she has said because I am weeping, knowing finally what this is about: gathering the people, telling the stories, sharing the bread, passing the wine. By the time Ellen passes the bread and cup to me, tears are running down both our faces, because she knows what it means for me finally to share in the feast.

And this is how the Christ comes. In the broken loaf and the spilled wine, yes, but also in the gathering, and the stories, and the tears, and the deep knowing of one person by another. This is how he comes, longing not for our brokenness but for our healing. This is how he comes, calling us to remember the people living in pieces and to cry out against their continual wounding. This is how he comes, bidding us to birth him anew.

With each of our breakings

you break,

and with each

of our woundings

your own wounds grow deeper.

Yet you hold

the pieces together

till we learn to make

the new connections,

and you guard

each throbbing wound

till we have had enough

of pain.

You remind us

that it is our delight you seek,

not our suffering.

And you tell us

it is not the wounds

that give us life,

but the tending of them

in each other.

And you say

it is not the breaking

that makes us whole

but the mending of the pieces

that brings us life anew.

AN ANGEL NAMED THELMA

She hangs on my wall: a heat-painted bronze angel, hands clasped in prayer as she hovers over a crescent moon. The day I moved here, I placed her at the doorway to the family room, the action my unspoken house blessing. She watches the threshold.

When I found her in Atlanta and brought her to my home there, I showed her to some friends who'd stopped in. "She needs a name," I said. "Thelma!" Sandra immediately offered, then instantly regretted it. "No," I said. "That's perfect!" Thelma. I thought of the Thelmas I had known (both of them). Thelmas were solid, immovable, stalwart, a little wild. They could tell stories to raise the hair on the back of your neck. They weren't afraid of aging; the years rooted them, grounded them, widened their vision as well as their girth. They could spit.

An angel named Thelma is not your average angel. She most definitely is not among the current rage of angels depicted as ephemeral, fragile, benign beings who look like they wouldn't hurt a flea. She hangs out with the sorts of angels we find in the Bible. Hardly benign, these angels were messengers of harsh news and bearers of surprising invitations. They might come with comfort, but they always came with a cost.

An angel named Thelma is what I need in this season: an uppity angel at my shoulder. Someone who can breathe fire. Who will remind me that being nice won't sustain me through the labor. Who will cry out with me in the birth pangs. Who will dispatch the dragon who waits to devour what is struggling to be born.

BLESS THEM

who wait with us

who labor with us

who cry out with us

BLESS THEM

who know our limits

who push us beyond them

who see us through

BLESS THEM

who call us to our strengths

who tend us in our weakness

who dress each ragged wound

BLESS THEM

who laugh in the face of convention

who weep for our own pain

who bid us come and live.

BORN AGAIN

Born again?
Oh yes
I was/am/long to be,
again and again;
to know the tracing
and retracing,
making and remaking,   renaming
shedding, unloosing,   of heart
and flesh
and soul;
to know
and see
and taste anew,
drenched in Wisdom's waters,
delighting in her spirit
continually.

Bless me

with the wisdom of the crone

who values every one

of her days

but who has not forgotten

in the core

of her aging flesh

the way in which

you make

all things new.

week five

BIRTHING SONG

Dancing in circles,
moving in cycles,
never quite knowing
just where
we'll come down;
unloosing and clasping,
bearing and gasping
in this laboring season
of the Great Round.

Each passage a birthing,
each birthing a blessing
we can't always see
for it leaves its own scars;
it makes and remakes us,
stretches and takes us
through dying of worlds
and emergence of stars.

From threshold
to threshold,
each time and each season;
in longing, in leaving,
in silence, in sound;
in fullness and plenty
or fallow and empty
we learn with each turning
in the Great Round.

I did not seek

this birthing,

but you have drawn me

into the passage;

and I am the one

who is bearing,

and I am the one

being born.

week five

So in my

longing

yearning

breaking

gasping

groaning

laboring

bearing

birthing

I am asking,

O God my midwife,

deliver me.

BY HAND

These are some of the best gifts. The ones made by hand. The webbed, woven circle that came from David in the Carolinas, with blessings and prayers uttered into every strand. The photograph of my beloved Moon Tree, taken by my father years ago before it fell, recently printed from its slide and matted and framed by him, now hanging on my home's threshold. The deep-hued afghan from Toby, reminding me of her warm, enveloping hugs. Brenda's painting of Mary in labor, a scene I'd never seen depicted, her face scrunched in pain as Joseph waits like a catcher behind the plate to receive Jesus.

These hands, too, trace the shape of incarnation. Reenacting the ancient cycle of creation from chaos, they lend form and flesh to the waiting spirit. Brooding over the face of the deep, they stir the waters and make anew.

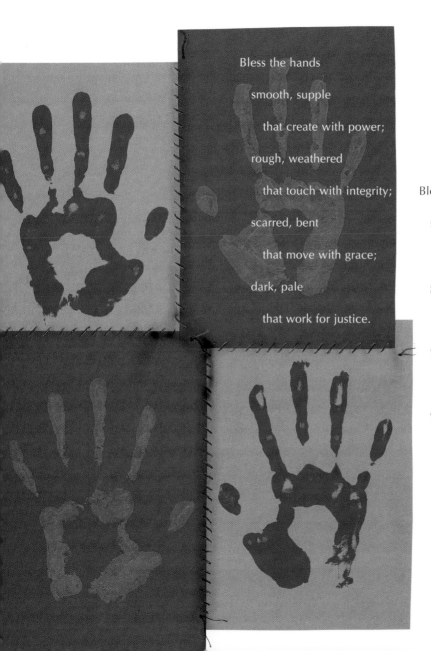

Bless the hands

  smooth, supple

    that create with power;

  rough, weathered

    that touch with integrity;

  scarred, bent

    that move with grace;

  dark, pale

    that work for justice.

Bless the hands

  shackled, free

    that point toward peace;

  graceful, longing

    that tend the weary;

  young, old

    that feed the children;

  yours, mine

    that move the world.

AFTER BIRTH

The first time I ever saw a placenta was in middle school, during one of our health units. A nurse brought it to our class-room—a sloppy red thing, I thought, in a plastic basin. We gaped, most definitely not having ever seen anything like this.

Afterward, I suppose, that particular piece of afterbirth went into the trash with other medical "waste." But I know places still exist in the world where those who attend the birthing will take the placenta and the umbilical cord and bury them in the ground. The newborn child becomes literally rooted in the soil as the earth is nourished. (If we did this, more of us, would we remember our kinship to the land we tread?)

On that day in middle school, I learned that the birthing woman has not reached safety until the afterbirth has wholly emerged. If any remains, she risks hemorrhage and death. The body cannot abide the unfinished business of birthing, the scraps and pieces left behind.

Neither can I. My body has never known the contractions of labor, but I know something of the effort of birthing, the ragged struggle to bring to light what lies hidden in my fertile darkness. I cry out to be delivered into wholeness, yet find myself vexed by the shreds left behind: the untamed memory, the ease with which a wound gives way. I grow impatient with how I must tend to the cleansing even after the birth, must continually mop up in the process of healing. Yet I know there will always be wounded places, that the labor of birthing has forever shifted my bones and altered my shape. We will long carry bits and scraps left in our tender inward places. It is left to us to discern how to name them, tend them, care for them so that they don't bleed us to death, don't waste us away unawares.

When we are spent

from the labor

and longing to rest

in our deliverance,

when we hunger

to stay

in the celebration

and crave

a lasting sabbath,

you tell us

this is where

our work begins.

For the labor

that is never over,

give us strength;

for the healing

that is ever before us,

give us courage.

May our resting

be for renewal,

not forever;

and may we work

for nothing

save that

which makes

your people whole.

WELCOMING

{ New Year's Day or

Second Sunday after Christmas }

Look around; they all gather together,
they come to you.

—Isaiah 60:4

I have friends arriving in two days. I have looked forward to seeing Pam and Marsha, and though I am not the most skilled host, I will at least spread fresh sheets on their beds in the guest room and make certain they have towels in their bathroom and put bagels and juice in the refrigerator for breakfast. It is easy to welcome these friends who have shared my journey in significant ways and in whom I readily sense the sacred.

But sometimes I do not welcome others so eagerly. I resist those who try my patience, or who drain my energy, or who seem so different from me that I become uncomfortable. Sometimes I see myself in the story that Kathleen Norris tells in her book *Dakota: A Spiritual Geography.* An old Russian Orthodox monk, trained to welcome all guests as Christ, tells a younger one, "I have finally learned to accept people as they are. Whatever they are in the world, a prostitute, a prime minister, it is all the same to me. But sometimes I see a stranger coming up the road and I say, 'Oh, Jesus Christ, is it you again?'"

Those who welcomed Jesus—the angels, the shepherds, the Magi—readily recognized him and knew the import of his arrival. They greeted him joyfully with their songs, their presence, their gifts. The rest of us sometimes have a more difficult time welcom-

If the Sunday for this week follows Epiphany, proceed to week 7.

ing Christ into our midst, particularly when he arrives in the guise of one who seems radically different from us or who gets under our skin or who angers us or who confronts us with parts of ourselves we don't want to see.

There are, at times, good reasons not to welcome one who appears in our path. Occasions arise when it becomes necessary to turn away from a stranger, to leave the house of an abuser, to close the door on an opportunity or relationship or dream. In so doing, we may learn what it means to welcome our own selves, to receive in a new way the wholeness God longs for us to know.

The Feast of the Epiphany, which most Christians celebrate on January 6, will soon be upon us. The word *epiphany*, from the Greek *epiphanos*, means "manifestation," "appearing," or "showing." As a holy day of celebration, Epiphany refers both to the appearing of Christ in the world and to the arrival of the wise ones who followed the star and welcomed the child.

As we prepare for Epiphany, God calls us to discern where the sacred shows forth, that we, too, may welcome it into our lives. The one who took flesh reminds us that to those with eyes and hearts to perceive it, the holy appears in our midst, in our lives, and in our own selves.

WISE WOMEN ALSO CAME

Wise women also came.
The fire burned
in their wombs
long before they saw
the flaming star
in the sky.
They walked in shadows,
trusting the path
would open
under the light of the moon.

Wise women also came,
seeking no directions,
no permission
from any king.
They came
by their own authority,

their own desire,
their own longing.
They came in quiet,
spreading no rumors,
sparking no fears
to lead
to innocents' slaughter,
to their sister Rachel's
inconsolable lamentations.

Wise women also came,
and they brought
useful gifts:
water for labor's washing,
fire for warm illumination,
a blanket for swaddling.

Wise women also came,
at least three of them,
holding Mary in the labor,
crying out with her
in the birth pangs,
breathing ancient blessings
into her ear.

Wise women also came,
and they went,
as wise women always do,
home a different way.

In this and every season

may we see them,

the wise ones

who come bearing

your gifts to us.

Give us eyes to see them now,

before they have left

They cloak themselves in garb

to go home some other way,

that rarely draws attention,

before we glimpse

but they are there

their departing shadows

 at the edge of the shadows,

edged in gold

in the margins of our days,

and smell their spiced perfume

on the threshold

lingering behind them

of our awareness,

in the air.

offering what we most need.

INCARNATION

—

She is returning from the birthing as I write. When Kary checked in with Bill last night, he said it might be two weeks now before Joann delivers. But I woke this morning, in this house in the woods of west Florida where I am visiting, thinking *today, perhaps today.*

The call came at noon. Kary, having offered to stay with Joann and Bill's daughter Alison during the labor, raced around the house in surprise. "What does one wear to a birthing?" I smiled, remembering my late-night mad dash to the hospital with Sally and Gordon when it came time to deliver my nephew Scott. Kary left. In jeans, maybe, or a cotton dress. I can't remember; she was a blur. She called several times during the day, and finally just now to say she is leaving. Kathleen has arrived via Caesarean section.

I sit at this borrowed desk, chewing on my pen, listening to the dogs shift in their sleep downstairs. I am trying to write about Advent and incarnation as Joann and Bill hold Kathleen and each other, touch her hands, her feet, her face. All I can write is *welcome, welcome, welcome.*

week six

Ancient One

who makes all things new,

may we receive with gentleness

and touch with hopefulness

and protect with fierceness

and love with tenderness;

and may we celebrate with gratefulness

and welcome with humbleness

and tend with gracefulness

all that you give

into our care.

THE WEDDING HOUSE

The family intended it as a mother-in-law house, but the mother-in-law ended up living somewhere else, and so the house in the woods became known as the wedding house when her grandson made plans to marry. The entire assembly processed there after the wedding, following the path of luminarias that had been laid out through the trees. It was a skeleton of a house, still in progress; tiny lights snaked along its frame, lending a glow to the thin covering stretched across it. Here they had laid the feast, prepared the celebration. Walking in, I found myself stunned by the grace of its incompleteness.

It was Advent eve when I drove home from the celebration, and the Seven Sisters danced in the night sky over my left shoulder all the way home. That night I dreamed that my bones were strung with lights, that my skin glowed in welcome, that within my skeleton a feast had been laid. Here was the wedding house, unfinished but waiting to celebrate the meeting of souls. Here were the guests, waiting to dance under the night sky.

O my soul,

this is your work:

to light the candles

set the tables

prepare the room

lay the feast

pour the wine

welcome the guests

and bless

in your innermost being

and celebrate

with your deepest delight

the lovers and friends

families and kin

and all who dare

to cast their lot together;

O my soul,

bless.

BREATHING LESSONS

Shallow breathing
is the plague
of the restless soul.
My hungry lungs
catch me unawares,
force me to feed them
with heavy sighs.

The scent of frankincense
and myrrh
arrives on the wind,
and I long
to breathe deeply,
to divine its trail.
But I know their uses
and cannot bring myself
to breathe deeply enough
to know
whether what comes
is the fragrant welcoming
of birth
or simply covers the stench
of death.

These hands
coming toward me,
is it swaddling they carry
or shroud?

And yet you remind us

that the wisdom

of the womb

points toward the truth

of the tomb:

that what contains us

for a moment

or a season

with your touch

will finally give way

to freedom.

Bless us,

that we may know

that which leads to wholeness;

that we may choose

the things

which make for peace;

and that we may welcome

the possibility

of our own release.

{day five}

My Own Fire

⟶

Sitting in the chapel, listening into the silence for long-absent voices, I catch your movement from the corner of my eye. I watch you pass the doorway but do not call your name, do not cross the threshold to greet you. It isn't spite that keeps me rooted, quiet, to my chair. And it isn't malice that leaves your rare missives unanswered. That would require more intent than I possess when it comes to you these days. My silence is not a door barred, simply one that I don't stand by anymore.

I wish you welcome at other fires, hope that other guesting doors beckon you across the threshold, hope even more that you learn what it means to welcome your own self. Me, I'm tending my own fire, finding its light more lovely than ever.

week six

When we have so diligently

welcomed one another

that we have neglected

to provide hospitality

to our own selves,

teach us

to be mindful

of the pilgrim

within our own souls

who longs

for a welcoming fire

and for shelter

in the dark.

SHELTER

—

In the house of Lesley and Linda there is always a spare room or at least an extra corner of a futon to curl up in for a spell. Often there is an abundance of knees to lean up against, and if your heart happens to be hurting at the time you drop in, they'll stop watching the game on TV long enough to give you a hug and feed you something.

Don't go if you're feeling complacent (or, perhaps, go as quickly as you can), because they tend to ask you questions that make you think, like what is the difference between boundaries and walls, and what would you call that dream if you had to give it a title? The best part is that they won't treat you like company. They assume you know where the tea and the kettle and the mugs are and that you'll make yourself a cup if you want one while you're sitting quietly reading on their sun porch. The other best part is when Lesley drives me all the way to the airport to fly home when she knows it would be okay just to drop me off at the MARTA station.

Come to think of it, there are a lot of best parts about visiting the house of Lesley and Linda. You really should go sometime.

Openness of hand

tenderness of embrace

spaciousness of heart

graciousness of home

blessedness of earth

vastness of sky:

for all the spaces

that bid me welcome

I give you thanks.

BELOVED
(f o r   p a u l)

"Here," she said, "in this here place, we flesh; flesh that weeps, laughs; flesh that dances in bare feet in grass. Love it. Love it hard."

—TONI MORRISON, BELOVED

Orion watches as we search for words of invitation, his piercing arrow poised over the exposed flesh of our soft throats. We have both of us come to this place of meeting emptied, hollowed out like the night sky above us, yet wise to the stars that blaze in our shadows. Years of illness have made you transparent in more ways than one, but flesh covers your bones just the same. We touch, skin to skin, a thousand messages passing in our meeting.

The hunter's arrow flies, but this time the piercing will leave not a gaping wound but a tender opening. This is the knowledge that I will carry within me in the days to come: that the ghosts in my bones, the ones that send their clomping echoes through my brain during sleepless nights, will cease their restless pacing; that the aching memories my body still carries will give way to new flesh. On the terrain of my skin, a new map emerges. With cautious fingers you trace the lines: Holy. Welcome. Beloved.

week six

You know the memories

that inhabit us

beneath the layers

of our knowing,

below the depths

of our awareness,

between the bones

that give us form.

Teach us to trust

those who will re-member us,

who will reveal to us

the blessedness

of our own flesh,

the belovedness

of our own beings,

and the possibility

of transformation

contained in each embrace.

week seven

THRESHOLDS

{ First Sunday after Epiphany }

His winnowing fork is in his hand,
to clear his threshing floor.

—LUKE 3:17

The foyer of my home is a sacred space. I spent hours stripping wallpaper from its walls, spackling and sanding, painting them in colors I liked. A table is there, on which I placed a stack of my favorite books and a pair of metal candlesticks forged in the shape of dancing women. On the wall hangs a photograph, made and framed by my father, of the Moon Tree, the wise old oak that once stood in the yard of my family's home and companioned me in my stargazing as I grew up.

This is my *threshold,* my entryway, the place where I choose what and who will come into my home. It is the space I pass through many times each day and will soon cross for the last time as I leave for a new job and a different home in a matter of weeks. I will have to learn again how to create a place of welcome, how to fashion a space where I will discern what and whom I invite into my life.

The word *threshold* originally referred to the doorway leading to the place where the threshing of grain occurred. Beyond the entrance lay the place of separating the wheat from the chaff, of sorting and sifting, of beginning to cull that which would become bread. John the Baptist used this image as he spoke of how Jesus would come to clear the threshing floor and gather the wheat. John's words served as a vivid warning to the people to prepare, to consider whether they were ready to walk through the doorway toward the life to which Jesus would call them.

We stand on the threshold of a new season. The Feast of the Epiphany, which we celebrate this week, is the Twelfth Day of Christmas and marks the end of this time of celebration. As we cross into the season beyond Epiphany, we are beckoned to ponder other passages we may be making. The thresholds of our lives serve as places to choose, to discern, to sort out what we consider important and where we feel called to go. We may find ourselves at a threshold by choice or by circumstance, arriving by our own design or landing there by events seemingly beyond our control. Whether or not it seems sacred at first, a threshold can become a holy place of new beginnings as we tend it, wait within it, and discern the path beyond.

In this season past, we have journeyed through darkness, desire, preparing a space, hope, birthing, and welcoming. We will know these places again and again in our lives because God's path unfolds not in a straight line but in a spiral. We emerge onto each new threshold with the experiences of the passage we have just made, but we will understand the journey past only as we continue to embrace the path before us. I come to understand the ways that the holy is born only as I enter the mysteries of Advent, Christmas, and Epiphany again and again. Each passage offers visions in the darkness. Each threshold offers signs for the way.

THRESHOLD DREAMS

The dreams came in the spring, weeks, maybe months, apart. We were in the foyer, the threshold of my home. That's all I remember, except that I was holding you. Looking back, I laugh in wonder. These are the dreams that threatened you? Standing there on the threshold. It made me crazy until I realized how much a person can fear an open door.

week seven

We do not all choose

the same place

of beginning;

not all doorways

are meant for entry.

And so

when silence falls

across the threshold

I have meant for welcome,

may you,

guardian of every passage,

cast your shadow

at my door.

THE DREAM OF THE DOOR

I come across a letter she wrote long ago, read again her words about the dream she had of building a door. *A beautiful wooden door,* she wrote. *Friends came by to help but it was my door—I was in charge and competent enough to build a door. And it wasn't a "keeping out" door but a "going through" door.*

I remember how, later, it was not her door that the intruder came through but the window. In the middle of the night he entered, in the shadows, taking dawn with him when he finally left.

We moved her to a new home, saw her to a new place behind security gates and up several flights. Her threshold was more difficult to get to now, but there she began to create it all over again. Windows may look less trustworthy these days, but there is still the dream of the door.

God of the threshold,

this we pray:

that what comes in

enters by consent,

by invitation

that what passes through

crosses over with grace,

with mercy

that what dwells within

resides in delight,

in integrity

that what goes forth

emerges for peace,

for blessing.

week seven

115

TWILIGHT'S TURNING

Sitting on my threshold
at twilight's turning,
door open,
arms around my knees,
wind through the entryway

here
I know
this is what I want:
not to be good
but to be whole.

week seven

You are there

in the way the light catches me

in my turning,

and in the way the wind moves me

in every step.

And in my resting

pausing

pondering,

in my quiet

wondering

stillness,

visit me with

your restless peace,

your laughter

on the wind.

FOR ST. ANNE, WHOSE SYMBOL IS THE DOOR

Who is also the patron saint of lost objects.
Whom we know only by legend.
Who was the mother of Mary.
Who became the grandmother of God.

Who must have taught her daughter
    something of boldness, of clarity,
    of passages, of the power of choosing,
    of not fearing angels
    or their wild propositions.

Who beckons me in this season
    as I seek my one threshold
    from many doors.

Whom I beseech:
    bless me for all my lostness
    light fire to my shadowy sight
    withstand my gut-born guessing,
    my passion for the night.

Hallow the endless hallway
    of doors lined frame by frame;
    guardian of the threshold,
    cry out my newfound name.

That we may know the power

to embrace

or to release

to welcome

or to turn away

to agree

or to dissent

to speak

or to keep our silence

to open

or to close

and to know each choice

that lies before us,

O God,

we pray.

A Bag of Many Colors

—

Brenda went to Peru last fall to visit a friend of ours. At Christmastime she gave me a bag she had brought back. Woven of brilliantly dyed thread into a bold Peruvian pattern, the bag is small enough to carry around my neck under a sweater when I travel or to put in a knapsack. At home I leave it on my dresser mirror, hanging by its long strap of braided yarn.

As I cross the threshold into a new season and a new year, the bag prompts questions. What do I need for the journey ahead? What would I put in the bag to take with me? What objects, words, blessings, hopes, charms would I keep within its colors against my chest as I meet the coming days? How will my actions in the year ahead stretch my own thresholds, my own boundaries, and bring me closer to others—to ones such as those who fashioned this very bag? Or do I need to leave it empty, to wait and see what will fill it this year?

Finally the bag is so full of questions that no space remains for anything else. Some say it will grow lighter with the journey, but though the contents may shift in handling, I think this bag will never be empty.

I cannot release the questions;

with every step they multiply,

and yet

they carry a wisdom

of their own.

God of mystery,

help me

to hold the questions,

lead me

to live them,

bless me

to bless them

for disturbing

my path.

week seven

M E D I C I N E   W O M A N
(f o r   s u e)

All during the dark year you kept the vigil light burning. When I lost track of the turning of seasons, you reminded me of the passage of time and that all had not remained idle beneath the terrain of my life. You might as well have been in another country for all the distance between our two coasts. But some things I held close, like memories of tables once shared and offerings that arrived from your far reach: native wine on my doorstep, a book in the mail, cards on which you inscribed words that helped tell me who I was on the days I had trouble remembering.

Three time zones to the east of you, I could call you in the middle of my night when the ghosts kept sleep at bay. Still awake, you uttered the charms that settled their troubled souls long enough to let me rest. *Use your voice,* you told me. *Know your anger,* you reminded me. *Anticipate resurrection.* Your words were a potent bundle I would place under my pillow. I'm hoping someday to give it back to you, my medicine woman.

week seven

For all that enfolds us

for each word of grace

and every act of care;

for those who offer refuge

for each shelter given

and every welcome space;

for the healing of our souls

for balm and rest

for soothing and sleep;

for vigils kept

and for lights kept burning;

blessed be.

THE CRAZY PIECES

—

An old, old quilt pattern, the crazy quilt . . . is a collection of scraps and snippets of leftover fabrics or remains of worn-out clothing stitched together. . . . The result is a wonderful hodgepodge of color and likely a quilt with memories in each patch.

—RACHEL AND KENNETH PULLMAN, THE WORLD OF AMISH QUILTS

There is nothing here that I want to forget, to throw away. Easier to toss it out, perhaps, or to bury it, but better to make it into something usable, something useful. Take the pieces and mold them into a bowl, say. Stitch the scraps together, make a bag that I'll come across periodically in a corner of my closet. Weave them into a prayer shawl. Turn them into a map. A puzzle. A book. Take the shards and fashion them into a glass window, stained, that forever changes the way light looks.

Make the pieces into a quilt, perhaps. A crazy quilt that seems to have no reason but has an ancient pattern all its own. I'll take every crazy scrap, stitch them together, wrap it around my shoulders, light the lamp. "Once upon a time," I'll say, knowing I could tell the story a hundred different ways, a thousand, and each telling would hold at least part of the truth, even as each patch contains part of the whole.

And so we take the ragged fragments

the patches of darkness

that give shape to the light;

the scraps of desires

unslaked or realized;

the memories of spaces

of blessing, of pain.

fragments

And so we gather the scattered pieces

the hopes we carry

fractured or whole;

the struggles of birthing

exhausted, elated;

the places of welcome

that bring healing and life.

And so we lay them at the threshold, God;

bid you hold them, bless them, use them;

ask you tend them, mend them,

transform them

to keep us warm,

make us whole,

and send us forth.